LEVEL 2

Rosa Parks

Kitson Jazynka

NATIONAL GEOGRAPHIC

Washington, D.C.

To all the kids who stand up for what's right. —K. J.

Copyright © 2015 National Geographic Society

Published by the National Geographic Society, Washington, D.C. 20036.

Trade paperback ISBN: 978-1-4263-2141-2
Reinforced library binding ISBN: 978-1-4263-2142-9

Editor: Shelby Alinsky
Art Director: Callie Broaddus
Editorial: Snapdragon Books
Designer: YAY! Design
Photo Editor: Lori Epstein
Production Assistants: Sanjida Rashid and Rachel Kenny
Rights Clearance Specialist: Michael Cassady
Manufacturing Manager: Rachel Faulise

The author and publisher gratefully acknowledge the expert content review of this book by Charles M. Payne, Ph.D., School of Social Service Administration, University of Chicago, and the literacy review of this book by Mariam Jean Dreher, professor of reading education, University of Maryland, College Park.

The publisher gratefully acknowledges the Rosa & Raymond Parks Institute for Self Development for their assistance in licensing the photos of Rosa Parks and in reviewing the contents and accuracy of this book.

Photo Credits
Cover, Library of Congress, used with permission of the Rosa & Raymond Parks Institute for Self Development, www.rosaparks.org; 1, Photo12/UIG/Getty Images; 3, USPS/AP Images; 4-5, Marion Post Wolcott/Library of Congress Prints and Photographs Division; 6, Bettmann/Corbis/AP Images; 7 (UP), Bettmann/Corbis; 7 (CTR), Jim McKnight/AP Images; 7 (LO), Bettmann/Corbis; 8, Buyenlarg/Getty Images; 9, Library of Congress Prints and Photographs Division; 10, Everett Historical/Shutterstock; 11, Schomburg Center for Research in Black Culture/The New York Public Library; 12 (UP), NY Daily News Archive/Getty Images; 12 (LO), Chris Ratcliffe/Bloomberg/Getty Images; 13 (UP), Underwood Archives/Getty Images; 13 (CTR), Corbis; 13 (LO), L.W. Hine/Library of Congress Prints and Photographs Division; 14, Keystone-France/Gamma-Keystone/Getty Images; 16, Underwood Archives/Getty Images; 17, National Archives/AP Images; 18 (UP), Don Cravens/The LIFE Images Collection/Getty Images; 18 (LO), Joseph Sohm/Corbis; 19, Horace Cort/AP Images; 20, Universal History Archive/UIG/Getty Images; 21 (UP), Underwood Archives/Getty Images; 21 (LO), The U.S. National Archives and Records Administration; 22-23, Bettmann/Corbis; 24 (UP), Manuscripts, Archives and Rare Books Division, Schomburg Center for Research in Black Culture, The New York Public Library; 24 (CTR), Bob Adelman/Corbis; 24 (LO), Carol M. Highsmith/Library of Congress Prints and Photographs Division; 25 (UP), Pete Souza/White House Photo/Getty Images; 25 (CTR LE), EPA/Olivier Douliery/ Pool/Alamy; 25 (CTR RT), Norm Dettlaff/Las Cruces Sun-News/AP Images; 25 (LO), William Philpott/Reuters/Corbis; 26 (BACKGROUND), simon2579/iStockphoto; 27, AP Images; 28, Joe Marquette/AP Images; 28 (BACKGROUND), simon2579/iStockphoto; 29, Kirthmon F. Dozier/TNS/Zuma Press; 30 (UP), Horace Cort/AP Images; 30 (CTR), Walter Bibikow/age fotostock RM/Getty Images; 30 (LO), Everett Historical/Shutterstock; 31 (UP), The U.S. National Archives and Records Administration; 31 (CTR RT), Carl Iwasaki/The LIFE Images Collection/Getty Images; 31 (CTR LE), Bettmann/Corbis; 31 (LO), Cameron Davidson/Corbis; 32 (UP LE), Bettmann/Corbis; 32 (UP RT), Keystone-France/Gamma-Keystone/Getty Images; 32 (CTR LE), Kirthmon F. Dozier/TNS/Zuma Press; 32 (CTR RT), Afro American Newspapers/Gad/Getty Images; 32 (LO LE), AP Images; 32 (LO RT), Bettmann/Corbis/AP Images; header, Milena_Bo/Shutterstock; vocab, Titova E/Shutterstock

National Geographic supports K–12 educators with ELA Common Core Resources.
Visit natgeoed.org/commoncore for more information.

Printed in the United States of America
15/WOR/1

Table of Contents

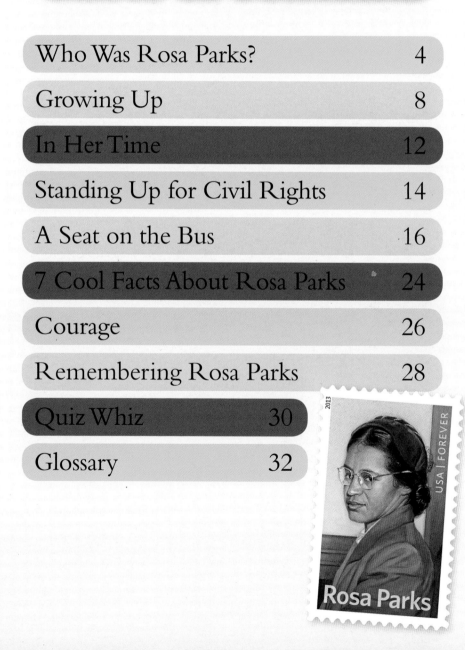

2013

USA / FOREVER

Rosa Parks

Who Was Rosa Parks?

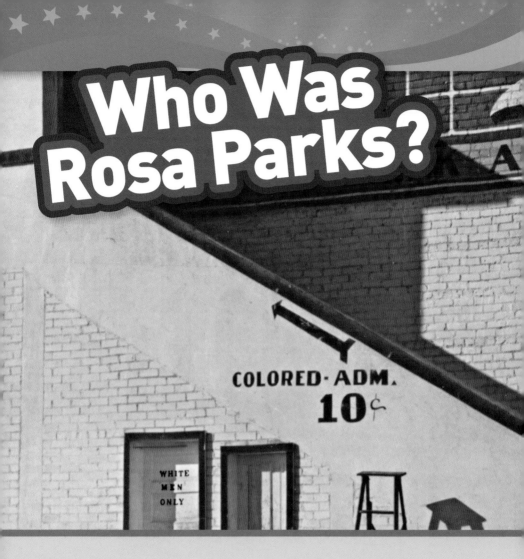

COLORED · ADM.
10¢

WHITE
MEN
ONLY

Can you imagine a world where
white children could ride a school
bus every morning, but black children
had to walk? Can you imagine a
world where black people couldn't

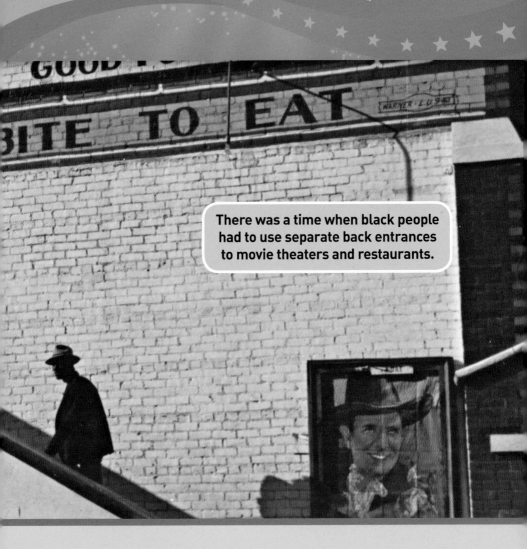

There was a time when black people had to use separate back entrances to movie theaters and restaurants.

drink from the same water fountains as white people or sit with them on a city bus?

This world was real. And it happened in the United States.

Some white people felt they should be treated better than black people. Segregation (SEG-rih-GAY-shun) laws were used to give more rights and a better life to white people.

Word to Know

SEGREGATION: the act of keeping a group apart from others

Rosa Parks helped change these unfair laws by thinking and acting. She stood up for herself and others her whole life.

In Her Own Words

"If I did not resist being mistreated . . . I would spend the rest of my life being mistreated."

Growing Up

Rosa Parks was born as Rosa Louise McCauley on February 4, 1913, in Tuskegee, Alabama.

She lived on a farm with her parents and grandparents. She was a small, quiet girl. She loved to read nursery rhymes and fairy tales like "Little Red Riding Hood." She also helped take care of her little brother, Sylvester.

an early portrait of Rosa

Nov. 1956

Rosa's grandparents were born as slaves. They taught her that all people deserve fair treatment. When Rosa was a child, slavery was over. But white people still had more freedom than black people.

Like the people pictured here, all black Americans were free in the 1920s. However, unfair laws made their lives difficult.

To help her parents pay for school after sixth grade, Rosa cleaned classrooms in the afternoon.

When she was 11 years old, Rosa moved to Montgomery, Alabama, to attend this school, the Montgomery Industrial School for Girls.

One day when Rosa was 11, a white boy pushed her. She pushed back. The boy's mother told Rosa she would go to jail. Rosa stood up for herself. She told them she didn't want to be pushed.

In Her Time

When Rosa was a girl in the 1920s, many things were different from how they are today.

TRANSPORTATION: White people and black people paid the same price to ride the bus, but they didn't have the same rules. White people could sit up front, but black people had to sit in the back.

MONEY: A chocolate bar cost 3¢. Today it costs about $1.35.

U.S. EVENTS: In 1920, women were allowed to vote for the first time in U.S. history.

TOYS AND FUN: Children played games like marbles and kick the can, which is similar to hide-and-seek.

SCHOOL: Many black children in the southern United States went to school only six months a year because they had to work in the fields to help their families. For the same reason, most black children didn't go to school past the sixth grade.

Standing Up for Civil Rights

When Rosa was 19 years old, she married Raymond Parks. They lived in Montgomery. She got a job as a seamstress in a department store. She sewed clothes to fit customers.

Like the people in this photo, Rosa Parks helped black people sign up to vote. There were many challenges. Parks herself tried three times before she was allowed to sign up to vote.

That's a
FACT!

Between 1945 and 1955, some Montgomery bus drivers wouldn't let Parks ride because she had a habit of refusing to give up her seat to white people.

Rosa Parks also worked to spread the word about civil rights. She attended meetings, rallies, and marches. She taught young people how to stand up for themselves. She helped people who were hurt by those who did not believe in civil rights. Standing up for civil rights was not easy. But Parks never gave up.

Word to Know

CIVIL RIGHTS: the rights of all people to be treated equally

A Seat on the Bus

On the night of December 1, 1955, Parks took the bus home after work. She sat down in a seat in the middle of the bus.

Parks riding a bus in Montgomery

After a few stops, the bus grew crowded. The driver asked Parks to stand so a white man could sit. She thought about the unfairness she'd faced all her life. She felt she had as much right to sit in the seat as anyone else, no matter the color of her skin.

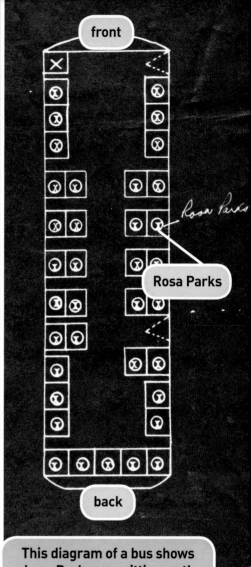

front

Rosa Parks

Rosa Parks

back

This diagram of a bus shows where Parks was sitting on the night of December 1, 1955.

Parks looked the driver in the eye.
In a quiet voice she answered, "No."

In Her Own Words

"I didn't even know if I'd get off the bus alive."

This is the bus Parks rode on December 1, 1955.

PLEASE
HAVE
EXACT
FARE
READY

2857

black and white passengers on a city bus

She must have been scared. Black people had been arrested for refusing to give up a seat on a bus. Some had even been hurt or killed for doing the same thing. People on the bus—black and white—feared what would happen.

The bus driver called the police. The police arrested Parks. At her trial, the court found her guilty of breaking a state segregation law. She was forced to pay a fine.

In Her Own Words

"People always say that I didn't give up my seat because I was tired, but that isn't true . . . No, the only tired I was, was tired of giving in."

7053

Name **Parks**
Surname
Alias
Nickname:
No. 79521 Co.

I. Thumb

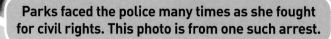
Parks faced the police many times as she fought for civil rights. This photo is from one such arrest.

Word spread about what had happened. Parks's act inspired people to stand up for fair and equal treatment.

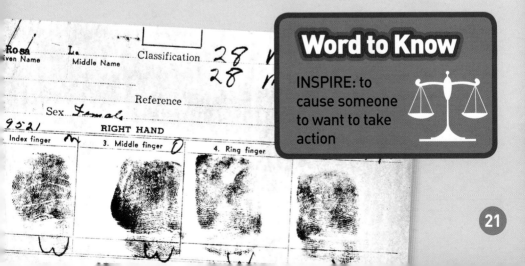

Ro sa
Given Name
L.
Middle Name
Classification 28
28

Reference

Sex Female
9521
RIGHT HAND
Index finger   3. Middle finger   4. Ring finger

Word to Know

INSPIRE: to cause someone to want to take action

Black leaders asked people to protest unfair rules by taking part in a bus boycott. A young preacher named Martin Luther King, Jr., made a speech. He urged people to stick together.

Words to Know

PROTEST: to say you don't agree with something

BOYCOTT: the act of refusing to use a service as a way to protest it

It was not easy for people to get to work and other places without the bus. But people kept the boycott going. It lasted more than a year. Finally, the Supreme Court ruled that everyone had the same rights on buses.

People boycotting the buses wave to an empty bus driving by.

7 COOL FACTS
About Rosa Parks

IF YOU NEED
A RIDE
Come To:
Anderson's Chapel
At: 816 Page Ave.
Anytime Between
6:00 AM. + 6:00 P.M.
REMEMBER !!!

1

Parks was not the first black person to refuse to give up a seat on a bus, but her actions sparked the famous bus boycott that helped change unfair laws.

2

Parks was part Native American.

In Montgomery, Alabama, you can visit the bus stop where police arrested Parks.

3

In 2012, President Barack Obama sat on the bus Parks was riding when she refused to give up her seat. The bus is on display at the Henry Ford Museum in Detroit, Michigan.

4

5

Today a statue of Parks stands in the U.S. Capitol Building in Washington, D.C.

When Parks died in 2005, bus drivers in Montgomery and Detroit honored her by reserving their front seats.

6

7

Many people call Parks the Mother of the Civil Rights Movement.

Courage

Parks paid a price for protesting. After her arrest, Parks and her husband lost their jobs. Angry people threatened them. Finally, in 1957, they left Montgomery and moved to Detroit.

In 1965, Parks took a job with a black congressman named John Conyers. For the next 20 years, she worked in Conyers's office.

1913

Born on February 4 in Tuskegee, Alabama

1924

Moves to Montgomery, Alabama, to continue school

1932

Marries Raymond Parks

Parks continued to stand up for civil rights. She attended meetings and peaceful protests. She even helped black people fight unfairness in other countries, like South Africa.

Parks protesting South Africa's unfair laws

Word to Know

PEACEFUL: without fighting or arguing

1955

Refuses to give up her seat on a bus and sparks a famous boycott

1956

U.S. Supreme Court rules that segregation on buses is unlawful

1957

Moves with her husband to Detroit, Michigan

27

Remembering Rosa Parks

Many people know about Parks's life because she refused to give up her seat on the bus that day in 1955. But now you know she spent her whole life standing up for fair treatment.

That's a FACT!

In 1996, President Bill Clinton awarded Parks the Presidential Medal of Freedom.

1965

Takes a job with Congressman John Conyers

1996

Awarded the Presidential Medal of Freedom at the White House

1999

Named one of the top 20 most important people of the century by *Time* magazine

Rosa Parks died on October 24, 2005, at age 92. After her death, she was given great honors, like the ones presidents and soldiers receive.

2005

Dies on October 24, at age 92

2006

Remembered with a statue in the U.S. Capitol Building in Washington, D.C.

2013

U.S. Postal Service creates a stamp in Parks's honor on what would have been her 100th birthday

QUIZ WHIZ

See how many questions you can get right!
Answers are at the bottom of page 31.

Segregation laws . . .

A. made sure kids went to school.
B. made sure all people could vote.
C. kept black people and
   white people apart.
D. kept people from driving too fast.

1

2

Where was Parks born?

A. Alabama
B. Michigan
C. Washington, D.C.
D. South Africa

Parks's grandparents . . .

A. died before she was born.
B. were born as slaves.
C. lived in a mansion.
D. owned a department store.

3

4

Parks stood up for civil rights by . . .

A. helping black people sign up to vote.
B. attending meetings, rallies, and marches.
C. teaching young people how to stand up for themselves.
D. doing all of the above.

What did Parks do when the bus driver asked her to stand?

A. She gave up her seat and stood.
B. She stayed in her seat to protest.
C. She got off the bus and walked.
D. She tied herself to the seat.

5

6

What happened during the bus boycott?

A. The bus ran out of gas.
B. People rode the bus for free.
C. Buses did not run.
D. People did not ride buses.

Why did Parks and her husband move to Detroit?

A. They wanted to retire.
B. She needed to care for her mother.
C. She wanted to return to her hometown.
D. They lost their jobs and were threatened.

7

BOYCOTT: the act of refusing to use a service as a way to protest it

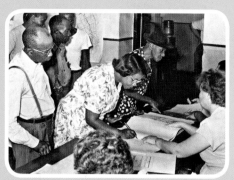

CIVIL RIGHTS: the rights of all people to be treated equally

INSPIRE: to cause someone to want to take action

PEACEFUL: without fighting or arguing

PROTEST: to say you don't agree with something

SEGREGATION: the act of keeping a group apart from others